BAZINGA!

First published in 2025 by OH
An Imprint of HEADLINE PUBLISHING GROUP LIMITED

1

Disclaimer:

Cataloguing in Publication Data is available from the British Library

ISBN 978-1-03542-243-2

Compiled and written by: Malcolm Croft
Editorial: Saneaah Muhammad
Designed and typeset in Avenir by: Andy Jones
Project manager: Russell Porter
Production: Rachel Burgess
Printed and bound in China

MIX
Paper | Supporting
responsible forestry
FSC® C104740

Headline's policy is to use papers that are natural, renewable and recyclable products and made from wood grown in well-managed forests and other controlled sources. The logging and manufacturing processes are expected to conform to the environmental regulations of the country of origin.

HEADLINE PUBLISHING GROUP LIMITED
An Hachette UK Company
Carmelite House, 50 Victoria Embankment, London EC4Y 0DZ

The authorised representative in the EEA is Hachette Ireland, 8 Castlecourt Centre, Castleknock Road, Castleknock, Dublin 15, D15 YF6A, Ireland

www.headline.co.uk   www.hachette.co.uk

THE LITTLE GUIDE TO
THE BIG BANG
THEORY
UNOFFICIAL AND UNAUTHORIZED

CONTENTS

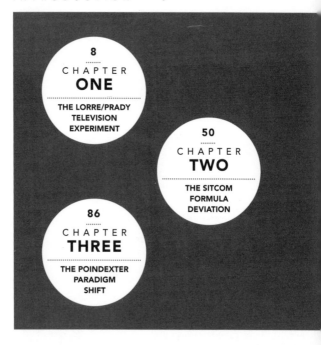

BAZINGA!

INTRODUCTION

Nearly fourteen billion years, give or take, after our whole universe became more than a hot, dense state, Chuck Lorre and Bill Prady's *The Big Bang Theory* exploded as a popular culture phenomenon. Today, a few years after its brilliant-if-heartbreaking 2019 finale, annual viewing minutes on Netflix and other streamers remain in the billions, showing no signs of slowing down. Just like the universal physical constant observed in the speed of light.

Running for 12 seasons from 2007, this witty, silly, infinitely quotable show, with its highly acclaimed ensemble cast, proved that prime-time TV about math, science and history didn't have to be a mystery to "the normals" (to quote Sheldon). Thanks to the award-winning chemistry between its principal characters – Leonard, Sheldon, Penny, Raj, Howard, Bernadette and Amy – *The Big Bang Theory* now regularly tops polls as the most bingeable comedy show ever made.

And deservedly so. It's bitchin'.

This indispensable *Little Guide to The Big Bang Theory* is the ultimate celebration; a tiny tome stacked with enough wit, wisdom and wisecracks to possibly kickstart wave-particle duality. Filled to the brim with the most memorable lines and a bunch of trivia, this compact compendium is guaranteed to boost your bookshelf's IQ with more "Bazinga's!" than is probably safe to consume in one sitting.

From Sheldon's petty awkwardness to Leonard's shy desperation and Howard's proud perversions to Penny's playful but pithy put-downs of all her new friends, *The Big Bang Theory* proves that Newton's laws of universal gravitation are true: it doesn't matter how big or clever we think we are, it is the connection between us that matters most.

It's time to get our Sheld-on, so let's go…

CHAPTER
ONE

THE LORRE/PRADY TELEVISION EXPERIMENT

Chuck Lorre and Bill Prady's vision for *The Big Bang Theory* was simple: reboot *Friends* for the internet age, but replace all the smug simpletons with even more smug, socially awkward (and sexually inept) scientists to create a smart comedy about modern relationships that didn't dare dumb down its intelligence for an audience.

The result? A sitcom that would have made Richard Feynman proud.

You wanna hear an interesting thing about stairs? If the height of a single step is off by as little as two millimeters, most people will trip. I did a series of experiments when I was 12. My father broke his clavicle.

Sheldon, to Leonard, about his earliest science experiments at home. This is not the reason Sheldon was sent to public school – that was for his "work with lasers"!

Season 1, Episode 1: "Pilot"
"Sheldon Cooper Quotes", the-big-bang-theory.com

Hey, look at me, I don't have a foreskin.

Raj, to Howard, mocking him for using his circumcision as a way to lure Missy, Sheldon's hot twin sister, into a date. It didn't work. (Missy seemingly had the hots for Raj though.)

Season 1, Episode 15: "The Pork Chop Indeterminacy"
"100+ *Big Bang Theory* Quotes That Are Outta This World", scarymommy.com, October 28, 2019

2311
North Los Robles
Avenue

The address of Leonard and Sheldon's apartment, in Pasadena, California.

They live in apartment 4a. Penny lives in apartment 4b.

I'm as much a part of this relationship as you two. I think that it is high time that we put all our cards on the table. For example, where is this going? Are you two ever getting married? And if so, where will we all live?

Sheldon, to Penny and Leonard, after not allowing the couple to have any privacy. The couple's lack of privacy is contributed to their inability to grow and make decisions together.

Season 7, Episode 13: "The Occupation Recalibration"
imdb.com

We don't need strength, we're physicists. We are the intellectual descendants of Archimedes. Give me a lever and a fulcrum and I could move the earth.

Leonard, to Sheldon, discussing a large box of furniture that they had to take up to their apartment on the fourth floor, with the elevator out of order.

Season 1, Episode 2: "The Big Bran Hypothesis"
"Sheldon Cooper Quotes", the-big-bang-theory.com

Wow, so in your world, you're the cool guys.

Penny, to Howard, after he told her that "Fishman, Chen, Chowdry, McNair aren't fielding a team in the University Physics Bowl this year," because "they formed a barbershop quartet, and got a gig playing Knotsbury Farm."

Season 1, Episode 13: "The Bat Jar Conjecture"
"100+ *Big Bang Theory* Quotes That Are Outta This World", scarymommy.com, October 28, 2019

"

I feel like Sheldon seems to approach every situation by trying to figure out the scientific nature of things. I like how his scientific reasoning so frequently doesn't work in the real world when he's dealing with Penny or when he's out in a restaurant – but he sticks to his guns. I really like that about him. He's very sure of himself in a lot of ways and I think that's very neat.

"

Jim Parsons (Sheldon), about portraying Sheldon, interview with Adam Tanswell, *Digital Spy*, October 5, 2011

Penny, Penny, Penny, Penny, Penny,
Penny, Penny, Penny, Penny, Penny,
Penny, Penny, Penny, Penny, Penny,
Penny, Penny, Penny, Penny, Penny,
Penny, Penny, Penny, Penny, Penny,
Penny, Penny, Penny, Penny, Penny,
Penny, Penny, Penny…

Sheldon, to Penny, while dressed in costume as
The Flash. When an angry Penny opens the door and asks
what the hell is wrong with him, his reply is: "I'm The Flash.
I just knocked 30,000 times."

Season 4, Episode 11: "The Justice League Recombination"
imdb.com

Sheldon changed the password. It's now 'Penny is a freeloader'... no spaces.

Leonard, to Penny, when she asks Leonard if their apartment Wi-Fi is not working. Rather than pay for her own, she borrows Wi-Fi from apartment 4a.

Season 4, Episode 14: "The Thespian Catalyst"
"Leonard Hofstadter Quotes", the-big-bang-theory.com

That movie was like twenty years ago. Imagine how saggy those things would be.

Howard, to Leonard, discussing the three-breasted Martian prostitute from 1990's *Total Recall* – a film that is, paradoxically, set in the future, the year 2084.

Season 3, Episode 9: "The Vengeance Formulation"
"*The Big Bang Theory*, Season 3", quotes.net

That's no reason to cry.
One cries because one is sad.
For example, I cry because
others are stupid, and that
makes me sad.

Sheldon, to Penny, who feels stupid while Sheldon is doing his very best to teach her about the basic fundamentals of physics.

Season 3, Episode 10: "The Gorilla Experiment"
"The Big Bang Theory: The 20 Best Sheldon Cooper Quotes", screenrant.com, November 27, 2023

I don't like to kiss and tell, but somebody made it to eighth base!

Howard, to Leonard, while entering Leonard's laboratory to tell him of his successful date the previous evening. Leonard, like the rest of us, is unsure what eighth base means in Howard's world.*

Season 3, Episode 12: "The Psychic Vortex"
tvfanatic.com, January 12, 2010

* It's seventh base with *his* shirt off.

Relationship Agreement,
Section 4: Boo-boos and ouchies.
You have to take care of it.

Sheldon, to Amy, regarding their contractual
"Relationship Agreement", after Amy fails to understand
why she needs to hear, or care, about Sheldon's splinter.

Season 5, Episode 10: "The Flaming Spittoon Acquisition"
"The Big Bang Theory, Season 5", quotes.net

It must be humbling to suck on so many levels.

Sheldon, to Leonard, after checkmating his roommate at three-dimensional chess.

Season 1, Episode 11: "The Pancake Batter Anomaly"
"*The Big Bang Theory*: Sheldon Cooper's 13 Best Quotes", movieweb.com, June 6, 2023

I want to build a road, but I need wood. Do either of you fellows have wood?… Oh, come on. I just want wood. Why are you making it so hard?

Sheldon, to Raj and Howard, while playing the board game Settlers of Catan, oblivious as to why his gameplaying companions are chuckling.

Season 5, Episode 13: "The Recombination Hypothesis"
imdb.com

My mom gave me the same lecture about my virginity. Gotta tell you, it was a lot more fun taking it out and playing with it.

Penny, to Sheldon and Leonard, comparing her virginity to a vintage mint *Star Trek* transporter toy she gifted to Sheldon after hearing that "it loses its value" once opened.

Season 5, Episode 20: "The Transporter Malfunction"
"Penny Quotes", the-big-bang-theory.com

Hang on, I know. He's the wheelchair-dude who invented time.

Penny, to Sheldon, excitedly, though incorrectly, admitting that she knows who Professor Stephen Hawking is.

Season 5, Episode 21: "The Hawking Excitation"
tvfanatic.com, April 5, 2012

You're right, all sex has is nudity, orgasms and human contact.

Leonard, to Sheldon, about sex, when Sheldon believes that Howard would choose Halo over sex because "As far as I know, sex has not been upgraded to include high-def graphics and enhanced weapons systems."

Season 1, Episode 7: "The Dumpling Paradox"
imdb.com

You do your little experiments, I do mine.

Penny, to Leonard, after serving Sheldon a couple of virgin Cuba Libres that "turned out to be a little bit slutty", just to see what would happen.

Season 1, Episode 8: "The Grasshopper Experiment"
"*The Big Bang Theory*, Season 1", quotes.net

Leonard, please don't take this the wrong way, but the day you win a Nobel Prize is the day I begin my research on the drag coefficient of tassels on flying carpets.

Sheldon, to Leonard, after Leonard asks: "Did UPS drop off a Nobel Prize with my name on it?"

Season 1, Episode 9: "The Cooper-Hofstadter Polarization"
"*The Big Bang Theory*, Season 1", quotes.net

Good news. Someone in this room gets to take a ride on a rocket.

Howard, to the group, after he receives a phone call from NASA asking him to go to space again.

Season 7, Episode 16: "The Table Polarization"
bigbangtheory.fandom.com

Oh sure! I sit on the floor for years, no one cares. The pretty white girl sat there for 10 seconds and suddenly we're all running to IKEA.

Raj, to the group, when Bernadette and Amy ask Leonard and Sheldon if they've ever considered getting a dining room table so they wouldn't have to eat on their laps.

Season 7, Episode 16: "The Table Polarization"
"Raj Koothrappali Quotes", the-big-bang-theory.com

You made an arithmetic mistake on page two. It was quite the boner.

Professor Stephen Hawking, to Sheldon, regarding Sheldon's thesis (you know, the one about the "Higgs boson being a black hole accelerating backwards through time").

Season 5, Episode 21: "The Hawking Excitation"
tvfanatic.com, April 5, 2012

If Bruce Banner is driving a rental car and turns into the Hulk, do you think it's covered, or does he need to add the Hulk as an additional driver?

Raj, to Howard, seemingly saying his intrusive thoughts out loud. Howard's response: "You really need a girlfriend."

Season 11, Episode 20: "The Reclusive Potential"
imdb.com

Ooh! That is PhD-licious. **„„**

Sheldon, to Penny and Leonard, after Penny orders a round of champagne (and a "packet of Splenda" for Sheldon) to toast Sheldon and Amy's publication of their super-asymmetry paper.

Season 12, Episode 1: "The Paintball Scattering"
"Sheldon Cooper Quotes", the-big-bang-theory.com

I slept with him. I married him. You want to bet against me?

Amy, to Raj, discussing whether or not Amy has the power to trick Sheldon into having babies with her.

Season 12, Episode 17: "The Conference Valuation"
"*The Big Bang Theory*: 10 Funniest Amy Quotes About Love", screenrant.com, January 25, 2020

Engineering – where the semi-skilled laborers execute the vision of those who think and dream. Hello, Oompa-Loompas of science.

Sheldon, to Howard, while visiting Howard at his engineering lab and introducing himself to Howard's colleagues.

Season 1, Episode 12: "The Jerusalem Duality"
"The Big Bang Theory, Season 1", quotes.net

Examining perturbative amplitudes in N=4 supersymmetric theories, leading to a re-examination of the ultraviolet properties of multi-loop N=8 supergravity using modern twistor theory.

Sheldon, to Penny, about what Sheldon was "otherwise engaged in" while everybody else got their driving license at 16.

Season 2, Episode 5: "The Euclid Alternative"
"The Man Who Gets The Science Right On *The Big Bang Theory*", npr.org, September 23, 2013

I know this is none of my business, but I just… I have to ask – what's Sheldon's deal? You know, like, what's his deal? Is it girls? Guys? Sock puppets?

Penny, to Leonard, regarding Sheldon's preference for romantic partners.

Season 2, Episode 6: "The Cooper-Nowitzki Theorem"
imdb.com

I'm very good at complaining.
If it were an Olympic Sport
I'd complain about what a stupid
sport it is, and then I'd take
home the gold.

Sheldon, to Penny, discussing the possibility of
complaining to the apartment landlord.

Season 10, Episode 7: "The Veracity Elasticity"
"*The Big Bang Theory* Recap: House of Lies", vulture.com,
November 4, 2016

Over the years we've formulated a number of theories about how he might reproduce. I'm an advocate of mitosis.

Howard, to Penny, about Sheldon's sexuality and preference for reproduction.

Season 2, Episode 6: "The Cooper-Nowitzki Theorem"
tvfanatic.com, January 20, 2009

Yeah, my parents felt that naming me Leonard and putting me in advanced placement classes wasn't getting me beaten up enough.

Leonard, to Penny, after Penny learns that Leonard plays the cello. Leonard being bullied at school is a leitmotif throughout his upbringing.

Season 1, Episode 5: "The Hamburger Postulate"
"Leonard Hofstadter Quotes", the-big-bang-theory.com

You actually had it right in the first place. Once again, you've fallen for one of my classic pranks. Bazinga!

Sheldon, to Leonard, delivering his first "Bazinga!" after teasing Leonard about an (in)correct equation he wrote on the apartment whiteboard.

Season 2, Episode 23: "The Monopolar Expedition"
"What Is the Secret Origin of 'Bazinga' From *The Big Bang Theory*?", huffpost.com, August 21, 2015

Good morning, everyone, and welcome to 'Science and Society'. I'm Dr Sheldon Cooper, BS, MS, MA, Ph.D., and Sc.D. OMG, right?

Sheldon, to his class, introducing himself via his own degree abbreviations. The fact that Sheldon knows the popular expression "OMG" is the real surprise.

Season 4, Episode 13: "The Love Car Displacement"
"*The Big Bang Theory*: The 20 Best Sheldon Cooper Quotes", screenrant.com, November 27, 2023

Yes, it tells us that you participate in the mass cultural delusion that the sun's apparent position relative to arbitrarily defined constellations at the time of your birth somehow affects your personality.

Sheldon, to Penny, when she introduces herself to Leonard and Sheldon as a Sagittarius, "which probably tells you way more than you need to know".

Season 1, Episode 1: "Pilot"
"Sheldon Cooper Quotes", the-big-bang-theory.com

❝

There's no point, I just think it's a good idea for a T-shirt.

❞

Sheldon, to Leonard, and the very first joke of the very first episode, as Sheldon and Leonard walk into a "High IQ" sperm bank. Sheldon's idea relates to the Double Slit Experiment, whereby a photon is directed through a plane with two slits in it and… well, you can look up the rest for yourself!

Season 1, Episode 1: "Pilot"
"Sheldon Cooper Quotes", the-big-bang-theory.com

Oh, look, there's the future Mrs. Wolowitz. No, wait, that's the future Mrs. Wolowitz, with her head in the lap of – eh, what a coincidence – the future Mrs. Wolowitz.

Howard, to the gang, who are all sat agog watching *America's Next Top Model*. Leonard replies: "Yeah, and they can all move in with you and your mother. The current Mrs. Wolowitz."

Season 2, Episode 7: "The Panty Piñata Polarization"
imdb.com

I'm sorry, but I'm not going to watch the *Clone Wars* TV series until I've seen the *Clone Wars* movie. I prefer to let George Lucas disappoint me in the order he intended.

Sheldon, to Leonard and Raj, while trying to agree on what to watch on TV.

Season 2, Episode 8: "The Lizard-Spock Expansion"
"*The Big Bang Theory* takes on *Star Wars* and *Star Trek*", techcrunch.com, November 18, 2008

Yes, well, I'm polymerized tree sap and you're an inorganic adhesive, so whatever verbal projectile you launch in my direction is reflected off of me, returns on its original trajectory and adheres to you.

Sheldon, to Leonard, after being teased. His response is a complex form of "I'm rubber and you're glue." (We think.)

Season 1, Episode 13: "The Bat Jar Conjecture"
"The Big Bang Theory, Season 1", quotes.net

The blunt instrument that will be the focus of my murder trial?

Leonard, to Sheldon, after Sheldon shows him Leonard's new girlfriend Dr Stephanie Barnett's Facebook page on his laptop screen, asking him, "Tell me what you see here?"

Season 2, Episode 9: "The White Asparagus Triangulation"
"Leonard Hofstadter Quotes", the-big-bang-theory.com

CHAPTER
TWO

THE SITCOM FORMULA DEVIATION

The last great prime-time sitcom (in front of a live television audience), *The Big Bang Theory* rewrote all the formulas and equations about what a comedy show could be in the digital era.

With whip-smart gags, puns and quips deployed as speedy as a neutrino, the show became a surprise hit among a wide demographic – from soccer moms to pre-teens – proving that having a genius-level IQ was not a pre-requisite to enjoy the plethora of sex jokes. Speaking of which…

I would very much like to read about your sex life. **"**

Sheldon, to Beverly Hofstadter, Leonard's mother, who wrote neuroscientific papers on hers and Leonard's father's sexual activity, or lack thereof.

Season 2, Episode 15: "The Maternal Capacitance"
"Season 2 Quotes", the-big-bang-theory.com

I don't know… how do carbon atoms form a benzene ring? Proximity and valence electrons.

Leonard, to Penny, when Penny asks about how Howard and Raj became friends with Sheldon.

Season 2, Episode 13: "The Friendship Algorithm"
"The Big Bang Theory, Season 2"*, quotes.net

It's very simple. Look. Scissors cuts Paper, Paper covers Rock. Rock crushes Lizard, Lizard poisons Spock. Spock smashes Scissors, Scissors decapitates Lizard. Lizard eats Paper, Paper disproves Spock, Spock vaporizes Rock and, as it always has, Rock crushes Scissors.

Sheldon, to Raj, explaining his rules for "Rock-Paper-Scissors" after the pair can't agree which *Star Trek* film is better – *Deep Space Nine* or *Saturn 3*.*

Season 2, Episode 8: "The Lizard-Spock Expansion"
"The Science Behind the Rules of Rock Paper Scissors Lizard Spock", wrpsa.com

* Simple subtraction will tell you that *Deep Space Nine* is six times as better.

Notify the editors of
The Oxford English Dictionary:
The word 'plenty' has been
redefined to mean 'two'.

Sheldon, to Leonard, after Leonard struggled to name
more than two women he's dated. "I've dated plenty of
women. There was Joyce Kim, Leslie Winkle…"

Season 2, Episode 2: "The Codpiece Topology"
"Sheldon Cooper Quotes", the-big-bang-theory.com

> **❝**
>
> I think a lot of what made Leonard and Penny work so well was my relationship with Johnny off camera, which turned into such sarcastic banter that bled into Penny and Leonard. Johnny and I's relationship, in a way, was mimicking Penny and Leonard. They were always giving each other shit, and Johnny and I have a similar relationship, which you do after years of being together.
>
> **❞**

Kaley Cuoco (Penny),
on Penny's relationship with Leonard (and her
off-screen relationship with Johnny Galecki), interview
with Jessica Radloff, *Vanity Fair*, October 3, 2022

I have eleven hours with her in a confined space. Unless she's willing to jump off a moving train and tuck and roll down the side of a hill, she will eventually succumb to the acquired taste that is Howard Wolowitz.

Howard, to Leonard, explaining his affection for *Firefly* actress, Summer Glau. Leonard responds: "My money's on tuck and roll."

Season 2, Episode 17: "The Terminator Decoupling"
imdb.com

Believe me, Howard, any girl who would be willing to play that, you don't want to see naked.

Leonard, to Howard, about Howard's great idea to "get some girls over here and play laser-obstacle-strip-chess".

Season 2, Episode 18: "The Work Song Nanocluster"
tvfanatic.com, March 17, 2009

Not with a thousand condoms, Howard.

Penny, to Howard, immediately regretting quantifying her hypothetical likeliness to have sex with Howard.

Season 2, Episode 19: "The Dead Hooker Juxtaposition"
tvgag.com

Good morning, Dr. Stephanie. I trust Leonard satisfied you sexually last night?

Sheldon, to Leonard, to Dr. Stephanie Barnett, a surgical resident, who uses her cunning in her fledgling relationship with Leonard.

Season 2, Episode 10: "The Vartabedian Conundrum"
avclub.com, December 9, 2008

I always thought when I finally settle down… it would be with someone… more like Megan Fox from *Transformers* or Katee Sackhoff from *Battlestar Galactica*.

Howard, to Penny, expressing his doubts about Bernadette, to which Penny retorts, "Are you high?"

Season 3, Episode 9: "The Vengeance Formulation"
"The Big Bang Theory, Season 3", quotes.net

I'm torn. She might be dying. I wouldn't want to miss that. On the other hand, if I let it go to voicemail, I could play it over and over.

Howard, to Bernadette, when Howard's overbearing mother calls. Bernadette is confused as to why her new boyfriend won't answer the call from his mom.

Season 3, Episode 5: "The Creepy Candy Coating Corollary"
"The Big Bang Theory Quotes", tv-quotes.com

Well, I'm a Slumdog astrophysicist.

Raj, to Abby, a Caltech science graduate student, who he met at a university mixer. Technically, due to Raj's parents' wealth, Raj is a Slumdog *billionaire* astrophysicist.

Season 3, Episode 12: "The Psychic Vortex"
imdb.com

In 2017, a *Big Bang Theory* spin-off was announced, a prequel, based on the childhood years of Sheldon Cooper, called *Young Sheldon*. It was an instant hit and ran for seven series until May 2024. The show was based on an idea that Jim Parsons had about Sheldon's small-town origins.

Following Young Sheldon's run, another spin-off was announced, *George & Mandie's First Marriage*, and is based on Sheldon's older brother, and tire salesman – George Cooper Jnr. The first episode aired in September 2024.

I don't need sleep. I need answers. I need to determine where, in this *swamp* of unbalanced formulas, squatteth the toad of truth.

Sheldon, to Bernadette, after having not slept in three days while trying to figure out why electrons behave as if they have no mass when traveling through a graphene sheet.

Season 3, Episode 14: "The Einstein Approximation"
"*The Big Bang Theory*, Season 3", quotes.net

Keep filling this one with babies, she's good.

Sheldon, to Howard, after Bernadette correctly diagnoses Sheldon's feeling: "Let's see… You're better than us, a little bit sorry for us, but mostly glad you don't have to be us."

Season 10, Episode 14: "The Emotion Detection Automation"
imdb.com

You know, both selective mutism and an inability to separate from one's mother can stem from a pathological fear of women. It might explain why the two of you have created an ersatz homosexual marriage to satisfy your need for intimacy.

Beverly Hofstadter, to Howard and Raj, about their close relationship. Howard's response is iconic: "Say what?"

Season 2, Episode 15: "The Maternal Capacitance"
"Beverly Hofstadter Quotes", the-big-bang-theory.com

That is my spot. In an ever-changing world it is a simple point of consistency. If my life were expressed as a function in a four-dimensional Cartesian coordinate system, that spot, at the moment I first sat on it, would be [0, 0, 0, 0].

Sheldon, to Penny, validating why it is his, and exclusively only his, spot on the sofa.

Season 2, Episode 16: "The Cushion Saturation"
imdb.com

> **"**
> It has been incredible to be part of a show that is so well written. Nerds are really scary when they get into large groups, you don't want to mess with them. So, it is good to have them on your side like we do.
> **"**

Simon Helberg (Howard),
on the show's nerd loyalty, interview with
Mike Gencarelli, *Media Mikes*, January 4, 2011

Well, today we tried masturbating for money.

Sheldon, to Penny, when Penny asks what the two scientists "do for fun", referring to the High IQ sperm bank that he and Leonard visited (unsuccessfully).

Season 1, Episode 1: "Pilot"
tvfanatic.com, January 16, 2009

You mock the sphincter, but the sphincter is a class of muscle without which human beings couldn't survive. There are over 50 different sphincters in the human body. How many can you name?

Sheldon, to Leonard, when Leonard refers to Sheldon's delight as a "yammering sphincter".

Season 4, Episode 2: "The Cruciferous Vegetable Amplification"
"Sheldon Cooper Quotes", the-big-bang-theory.com

I couldn't ride a bicycle because my mother was afraid I'd hit a bump and lose my virginity. **"**

Bernadette, to Howard, when comparing their overbearing mothers.

Season 3, Episode 5: "The Creepy Candy Coating Corollary"
"The Big Bang Theory, Season 3", quotes.net

My limbic system wants to take your pants off.

Penny, to Leonard, leading him out of apartment 4a in a bid to show Sheldon's assistant Alex, who is crushing on Leonard, that he is off the singles market.

Season 6, Episode 3: "The Higgs Boson Observation"
imdb.com

In all the years I've known him, he's never had the opportunity to receive my admiration.
I was excited to see the look on his face when it finally happened.

Sheldon, to Amy, about being unable to see Howard's delayed return to Earth following his time astronaut-ing in space.

Season 6, Episode 4: "The Re-Entry Minimization"
"*The Big Bang Theory*, Season 6", quotes.net

You sure that's your choice? 'Cause I've had that dinner.

Penny, to Sheldon, after Sheldon confirms "The person I'd most like to have dinner with is myself. I just don't see how I could disappoint."

Season 6, Episode 3: "The Higgs Boson Observation"
imdb.com

Whatever. Put us on the internet. I've always wanted a wedding with a comments section.

Penny, to Leonard, after being given a selection of wedding venue packages that offer to stream the whole event live on the internet.

Season 9, Episode 1: "The Matrimonial Momentum"
tvfanatic.com, September 22, 2015

I did Sudoku before they took it so I'd be ripped. And it's not just an MRI. The orbitofrontal cortex is lit up because I was thinking of you.

Sheldon, to Amy, about a functional MRI of his brain he had done, and, arguably, the most romantic thing he's ever said to Amy.

Season 10, Episode 11: "The Birthday Synchronicity"
imdb.com

"

I guess that makes me large breasts.

"

Howard, to Penny, in his typical seedy style, after Penny says: "It is the things you love that make you who you are."

Season 1, Episode 14: "The Nerdvana Annihilation"
"Howard Wolowitz Quotes", the-big-bang-theory.com

You tell people I'm a rocket scientist?! I'm a theoretical physicist. My God! Why don't you just tell them I'm a toll taker at the Golden Gate Bridge! Rocket scientist, how humiliating!

Sheldon, to Missy, his twin sister, after she informs him that she brags about her brother being a "rocket scientist" back home in Galveston, Texas.

Season 1, Episode 15: "The Pork Chop Indeterminacy"
tvgag.com

When I lie through my teeth to a woman, you nod and agree.

Raj, to Sheldon, at a Caltech mixer, where Raj meets Abby.

Season 3, Episode 12: "The Psychic Vortex"
imdb.com

You want something stupid, or you did something stupid?

Bernadette, to Howard, after Howard tries to butter his beautiful wife up with flattery. Bernadette's natural suspicion is that Howard is cheating on her… with Raj.

Season 10, Episode 17: "The Comic-Con Conundrum"
"Bernadette Rostenkowski-Wolowitz Quotes", the-big-bang-theory.com

---

You can't have your head shoved in a toilet as much as I did and not pick up a few things about plumbing.

Leonard, to Penny and Amy, regarding a burst pipe in the apartment building.

Season 10, Episode 4: "The Cohabitation Experimentation"
tvfanatics.com, October 11, 2016

A Catholic girl like you, wearing a big cross like that, might just give my mother the big brain aneurysm I've been hoping for.

Howard, to Bernadette, inviting her over to his (mother's) house for Shabbat with Mrs. Wolowitz, the stereotypical Jewish archetype.

Season 3, Episode 5: "The Creepy Candy Coating Corollary"
"The Big Bang Theory, Season 3", quotes.net

Are you kidding? You brought fancy wine and made fondue. I've slept with guys for less. It's a joke… based on real events.

Penny, to Raj, who shares his embarrassment about crashing the girls' night with Penny, Amy and Bernadette.

Season 10, Episode 18: "The Escape Hatch Identification"
tvfanatic.com, March 10, 2017

66

We're the same blood type, he knew he could harvest an organ.

99

Amy, to Raj, about what really first attracted Sheldon to Amy, contradicting his original response: "So many things. Her mind, her kindness and especially her body."

Season 10, Episode 21: "The Separation Agitation"
"The Big Bang Theory recap: 'The Separation Agitation'", *Entertainment Weekly*, April 13, 2017

CHAPTER
THREE

THE POINDEXTER PARADIGM SHIFT

The Big Bang Theory's arrival and success in popular culture was serendipitous. It was a time when twenty-something tech nerds not only ruled the world with their innovations, but were also now considered cooler than cool, displacing the jocks and beauty queens for the first time in American history.

This is known as the "Poindexter Paradigm Shift", so those at the back of the class, pay attention…

Well, now, did you also have a dog? Because I found what appears to be a battery-operated chew toy.

Sheldon, to Penny, after rummaging through her closet and discovering a dead goldfish and (what appears to be) a vibrator.

Season 6, Episode 19: "The Closet Reconfiguration"
imdb.com

Never knocked on my own door before. That was a wild ride.

"

Sheldon, to Amy, after knocking nine times on his apartment door, hoping that Amy, his new roommate, would let him in.

Season 6, Episode 23: "The Love Spell Potential"
"Quotes from 'The Love Spell Potential'", the-big-bang-theory.com

Sex criminals don't have keys, Ma!

99

Howard, to Mrs. Wolowitz, his mother, as he unlocks the front door and Mrs. Wolowitz yells, "Who's there?! Are you a sex criminal?!"

Season 4, Episode 16: "The Cohabitation Formulation"
"*Big Bang's* Best Recurring Characters", tvline.com, May 16, 2019

It was not a crisis. Apparently I favoured the left one. She got a little lopsided.

Leonard, to Penny, about his mother's new book, *The Disappointing Child* by Beverly Hofstadter, and more specifically, the chapter on the "breastfeeding crisis".

Season 7, Episode four: "The Raiders Minimization"
"Penny Quotes", the-big-bang-theory.com

Sheldon, we are in a relationship. When you get angry, tell me. You don't need to seek revenge.

Amy, to Sheldon, after Amy ruined *Raiders of the Lost Ark* for Sheldon, by pointing out its "glaring story problem".*

Season 7, Episode 4: "The Raiders Minimization".
imdb.com

* "Indiana Jones plays no role in the outcome of the story. If he weren't in the film, it would turn out exactly the same," Amy clarifies, upsetting Sheldon greatly. Amy does have a point, to be fair.

66

It's awesome to be on a prime-time TV show, but I think the best thing is the cast, who I love, and the producers, our directors, and we're having such a good time because we love each other and that speaks to the amount of fun we're having.

99

Kunal Nayyar (Raj),
on the cast's enjoyment of making the show,
interview with Matt Goldberg, *Collider*,
August 18, 2008

Have I ever told you you're like a sexy praying mantis?

Amy, to Sheldon, while drunk, telling Sheldon how she really feels about his looks.

Season 6, Episode 1: "The Date Night Variable"
tvgag.com

Amy, when I look in your eyes and you're looking back in mine, everything feels not quite normal because I feel stronger and weaker at the same time. I feel excited and, at the same time, terrified. The truth is, I don't know what I feel, except… I know what kind of man I want to be.

Sheldon, to Amy, stealing a line from "the first *Spider-Man* movie".

Season 6, Episode 1: "The Date Night Variable".
"*The Big Bang Theory*: Sheldon Quotes *Spider-Man*", comicbook.com, September 27, 2012

I would ask you guys if you wanted dessert, but I know Sheldon doesn't eat dessert on Tuesdays, and even if Raj wanted something, he couldn't tell me. Howard won't order anything, but he will come up with some sort of skeevy comment involving the words 'pie' or 'cheesecake', and Leonard is lactose intolerant, so he can't eat anything here without his intestines blowing up like a balloon animal. **"**

Penny, to the group, as she serves them at The Cheesecake Factory, where she works. A perfect summary of her scientist friends and their particular, peculiar flaws.

Season 4, Episode 4: "The Hot Troll Deviation"
"13 *Big Bang Theory* Quotes That Prove Penny Was Actually The Smartest", screenrant.com, August 30, 2022

My point is, I don't like when things change. So, regardless of your feelings, I would like you to continue dating Leonard. And also, while we're on the subject, you recently changed your shampoo. I'm not comfortable with the new scent. Please stop this madness and go back to green apple.

Sheldon, to Penny, offering his advice on both dating and hair products at the same time.

Season 6, Episode 2: "The Decoupling Fluctuation"
"Sheldon Cooper Quotes", the-big-bang-theory.com

Oh, you poor thing. Is having a real-life girlfriend who has sex with you getting in the way of your board games?

Penny, to Leonard, after Leonard whines that he doesn't spend as much time playing "*Dungeons and Dragons* with the guys" anymore.

Season 6, Episode 1: "The Date Night Variable"
"*The Big Bang Theory*: Sheldon Quotes *Spider-Man*", comicbook.com, September 27, 2012

Hang on. Are you feeling insecure? Because that's my thing, and if you take it away, I don't know what I'm bringing to this relationship.

Leonard, to Penny, after Leonard tells Penny that Alex, Sheldon's attractive assistant, made a flirty and suggestive pass at Leonard.

Season 6, Episode 12: "The Egg Salad Equivalency"
imdb.com

Shhhh! You can't ask a question like that in here! You trying to start a rumble!?

Stuart (Bloom), to Amy, at the comic book store, after she asks: "Who's the best superhero?"

Season 6, Episode 13: "The Bakersfield Expedition"
"*The Big Bang Theory*: The 10 Best Comic Book Quotes For Nerds", screenrant.com, December 13, 2019

It's why I never open a door without knocking three times. The first one's traditional, but two and three are for people to get their pants on.

Sheldon, revealing that knocking nine times in three bursts on people's doors began when he was sent home early from college (aged 13!) to find his father in bed with another woman.

Season 10, Episode 5: "The Hot Tub Contamination"
"*The Big Bang Theory's* Sheldon Cooper has stopped knocking on doors three times and no one knows why", metro.co.uk, November 15, 2018

Amy pointed out that between the two of us, our genetic material has the potential of producing the first in a line of intellectually superior, benign overlords to guide humanity to a brighter tomorrow.

Sheldon, to Penny, after Amy's sudden and frank invitation to Sheldon to reproduce a child together.

Season 4, Episode 1: "The Robotic Manipulation"
tvfanatic.com, September 24, 2010

If it wasn't for this beer I couldn't even talk to you right now. I'm a wreck. There are many things seriously wrong with me. And not quirks either. Like diagnosable psychological problems. Maybe brain damage. Go out with me on one date and I promise you you'll see.

Raj, to Lucy, a girl he meets at a singles-only Valentine's Day party held in the comicbook store. (She ends up giving him her number!)

Season 6, Episode 17: "The Monster Isolation"
"Raj Koothrappali Quotes", the-big-bang-theory.com

Leonard, I'm a physicist, not a hippie.

Sheldon, to Leonard, after Leonard asks him, "Well, have you considered telling her how you feel?"

Season 4, Episode 5: "The Desperation Emanation"
"*The Big Bang Theory*: 'The Desperation Emanation' Review", ign.com, May 5, 2012

Well, word around the university is I'm giving her sex organs a proper jostling.

Sheldon, to Penny, discussing his and Amy's physical relationship reputation on campus when Penny asks "What's the deal?" with them having physical intimacy (or not).

Season 6, Episode 14: "The Cooper/Kripke Inversion"
"The Big Bang Theory, Season 6", quotes.net

Oh, sweetie. If you're going to do anything to screw things up, it's going to be while you're here, not while you're away.

Penny, to Leonard, upon hearing the news that Leonard will be going on a three-month research expedition to the North Sea with Professor Stephen Hawking and was nervous about screwing up what he had with Penny.

Season 6, Episode 24: "The Bon Voyage Reaction"
imdb.com

Sheldon is the smartest person I've ever met. He's a little broke and he needs me. I guess I need him, too.

Leonard, to Professor Proton, after Leonard likened the good traits of Sheldon to that of a dog.

Season 7, Episode 7: "The Proton Displacement"
"The Big Bang Theory, Season 7", quotes.net

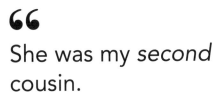

66

She was my *second* cousin.

99

Howard, to Raj and a group of friends at Howard's Bachelor party, after Raj's announcement that Howard lost his virginity to his cousin.

Season 5, Episode 22: "The Stag Convergence"
"Quotes from 'The Stag Convergence'", the-big-bang-theory.com

Sheldon went up to him afterwards and said, 'Maybe if you weren't so distracted by sick children in Africa you could have put a little more thought into Windows Vista.'

Raj, telling Priya, his sister, about the time Microsoft founder Bill Gates punched Sheldon in the face.

Season 4, Episode 17: "The Toast Derivation"
"Microsoft mogul Bill Gates set to cameo on *The Big Bang Theory*", dailymail.com, February 21, 2018

Other than my mother, my sister and my mee-maw, no. But in the interest of full disclosure, I was once on a bus and had to give mouth-to-mouth resuscitation to an elderly nun who passed out from heat exhaustion. Every year I get a Christmas card from her, signed with far too many X's and O's.

Sheldon, to Penny, Bernadette and Amy, after Penny asks: "Have you ever kissed a girl?"

Season 4, Episode 21: "The Agreement Dissection"
bigbangtheory.fandom.com

Leonard's mom wouldn't give him any sort of approval growing up. It makes him desperate to please women. That's why the foreplay goes on and on.

Penny, to Priya, Raj's sister and Leonard's new girlfriend, discussing Leonard's desire to outperform foreplay.

Season 4, Episode 23: "The Engagement Reaction"
imdb.com

I study the brain, the organ responsible for Beethoven's 'Fifth Symphony'. Bernadette studies yeast, the organism responsible for Michelob Lite.

Amy, to Sheldon, who fails to see the distinction between Amy's doctorate in neurobiology to Bernadette's PhD in microbiology.

Season 4, Episode 24: "The Roommate Transmogrification"
"The Big Bang Theory, Season 4", quotes.net

You can't ruin a friendship with sex. That's like trying to ruin ice cream with chocolate sprinkles.

Raj, to Penny, after they sleep together and Penny says: "We should have never slept together. It's what ruins friendships."

Season 5, Episode 1: "The Skank Reflex Analysis"
The Big Bang Theory: Penny Hofstadter's 10 Best Quotes", movieweb.com, June 23, 2023

Get your women in line! You make them apologize to Amy and set things right! I am a man of science, not someone's snuggle bunny!

Sheldon, to Howard and Leonard, after Amy was left out of their wedding shopping plans, forcing Sheldon to comfort-spoon Amy all night.

Season 5, Episode 8: "The Isolation Permutation"
"Sheldon Cooper Quotes", the-big-bang-theory.com

> **"**
>
> One of the benefits of having a show run this long is that we really have gotten to see these characters evolve in a very organic way. And it evolved into this show about the beauty of human potential, in a way, because these characters have had a chance to grow up and the fact that they've all sort of become the best possible version of themselves and done things that they wouldn't necessarily have seen themselves doing before.
>
> **"**

Melissa Rauch (Bernadette),
on the longevity of the show and the character's evolution, interview with Erin Clements, *Today*,
April 25, 2019

New topic: Women.
Delightfully mysterious, or
batcrap crazy?

Sheldon, to the gang, discussing Amy's "estrogen-fueled need to page through thick glossy magazines that make me hate my body".

Season 5, Episode 8: "The Isolation Permutation"
tvfanatic.com, November 3, 2011

When I first came to this country, I didn't know how to behave, or how to dress, or what was cool, I was pretty lonely. But, then I met Howard and suddenly my life changed, because we could be lonely together. This man became my whole world!

Raj, to Howard, during his drunk best man's speech at Howard's bachelor party.

Season 5, Episode 22: "The Stag Convergence"
"The Big Bang Theory: 10 Quotes That Perfectly Sum Up Raj As A Character", screenrant.com, September 1, 2022

In a way, we've kind of been involved in a five-year experiment.

Penny, to Alex Jensen, a Caltech physics doctoral student and Sheldon's assistant, after Alex asks Penny if she knows Leonard.

Season 6, Episode 3: "The Higgs Boson Observation"
"The Big Bang Theory, Season 6", quotes.net

Okay, well, thanks for the nightmares.

Penny, to Leonard and Howard, after Leonard suggests, "I think Sheldon might be the larval form of his species and someday he'll spin a cocoon and emerge two months later with moth wings and an exoskeleton."

Season 2, Episode 6: "The Cooper-Nowitzki Theorem"
"Leonard Hofstadter Quotes", the-big-bang-theory.com

You know what? If it's creepy to use the internet, military satellites and robot aircraft to find a house full of gorgeous young models so that I can drop in on them unexpectedly, then fine, I'm creepy.

Howard, to Raj and Leonard, after discovering the location of the house that appeared on the reality TV show, *America's Next Top Model*.

Season 2, Episode 7: "The Panty Piñata Polarization"
imdb.com

In the winter, that seat is close enough to the radiator to remain warm, and yet not so close as to cause perspiration. In the summer, it's directly in the path of a cross-breeze created by opening windows there and there. It faces the television at an angle that is neither direct, thus discouraging conversation, nor so far wide as to create a parallax distortion. I could go on.

"

Sheldon, to Penny, offering geometrically relevant facts to Penny about his "spot" on the sofa in apartment 4a. The exclusivity of Sheldon's particular spot is a series-long running joke and is a visual metaphor for Sheldon's social peculiarities.

Season 1, Episode 1: "Pilot"
"Sheldon Cooper Quotes", the-big-bang-theory.com

Ladies, please. These four walls once housed an intellectual salon where the mind received nourishment as well as the stomach. But through no one's fault… Penny… the quality of dinner conversation in this apartment has declined. And again, I'm looking at no one in particular… Penny.

Sheldon, to Bernadette, Penny and Amy, who are thoroughly unimpressed with the intellectualism of their colloquial dinner conversation.

Season 5, Episode 8: "The Isolation Permutation"
imdb.com

Now listen here, Sheldon, I've been telling you since you were five years old, it's okay to be smarter than everyone else… but you can't go around pointing it out!

Mary, Sheldon's mother, trying to get Sheldon to apologize to his boss, Dr. Gablehauser. Sheldon later reluctantly apologizes: "We may have gotten off on the wrong foot when I called you an idiot. I was wrong… to point it out."

Season 1, Episode 4: "The Luminous Fish Effect"
"*The Big Bang Theory*, Season 1", quotes.net

I don't use my nipples either, maybe they should reassign those.

Sheldon, to Howard and Raj, after Raj tells Sheldon that his car parking spot has been reassigned to Howard following his return to space because Sheldon doesn't use it as he can't drive.

Season 6, Episode 9: "The Parking Lot Escalation"
"Sheldon Cooper Quotes", the-big-bang-theory.com

I bet that started off as a joke, but by the third one, you realized there was something strangely enjoyable about it.

Sheldon, to Penny, after Penny knocks nine times on Sheldon's door and realizes how much fun it is to get her own back after all these years.

Season 8, Episode 21: "The Communication Deterioration"
"*The Big Bang Theory*'s Steve Molaro Now Regrets Adding Sheldon's Knocking Habit", looper.com, December 1, 2022

I feel five pounds lighter. 🙶

Amy, to Bernadette and Penny, after enduring her first bikini wax, an event that seemingly took forever and removed an eye-watering amount of pubic hair.

Season 6, Episode 9: "The Parking Lot Escalation"
"Kaley Cuoco Opens Up About Her 'Yoga Body'", yahoo.com, August 30, 2017

No one ever bought me drinks at a bar because my brain just popped out of my shirt.

Penny, to Amy, after Amy tells Penny that "Some people think the sexiest organ is the brain."

Season 9, Episode 8: "The Mystery Date Observation"
"*The Big Bang Theory*: 15 Best Penny Quotes", screenrant.com

CHAPTER
FOUR

THE BAZINGA APPRECIATION PHENOMENON

A huge hit from the outset, *The Big Bang Theory* has created a multiverse of possibilities for the future, including at least two spin-offs, countless comics and merchandise and worldwide syndication.

It also rocketed its lead actors into the low Earth orbit of fame and fortune, with the cast earning record-setting salaries per episode, as well as a legion of loyal "Bangers" (the name of the show's fans, probably).

Get your "Bazinga's" ready, we're about to go punchline hunting…

It's like that science thing.
For every action you have
a gigantic and annoying
reaction.

Penny, to Leonard, discussing Raj moving into
Sheldon's room in apartment 4a, and Sheldon
being acceptable to it.

Season 10, Episode 18: "The Escape Hatch Identification"
tvfanatic.com, March 10, 2017

I find the notion of romantic love to be an unnecessary cultural construct that has no value to human relationships. I trust this clarification allows us to return to boy-slash-friend-slash-girl-slash-friend status?

Amy, to Sheldon, strangely validating her feelings for Sheldon. Sort of. It's precisely this kind of sexy talk that motors Sheldon's boat.

Season 4, Episode 5: "The Desperation Emanation"
"*The Big Bang Theory*, Season 4", quotes.net

Oh, I stopped that, it was dumb. Uni, bi, tri, menstrual, all cycles are dumb.

Sheldon, to Amy, when Amy asks Sheldon: "What about learning the unicycle?" Amy later apologizes to Sheldon for calling him a quitter.

Season 11, Episode 3: "The Cognition Regeneration"
"Sheldon Cooper Quotes", the-big-bang-theory.com

66
If I find my foreskin, I'm gonna kill myself.
99

Howard, to Bernadette, after they go through Howard's childhood memory box and find items such as the boutonnière from his high school prom and a piece of cake from his Bar Mitzvah.

Season 8, Episode 18: "The Leftover Thermalization"
tvfanatic.com, March 13, 2015

> **Hey, what up, science bitches?**

Howard, to Leonard, Sheldon and Raj, while accompanied by his very attractive – and very tall – date at a university mixer. The gang are suspicious.

Season 1, Episode 4: "The Luminous Fish Effect"
imdb.com

A more plausible explanation is that his work in robotics has made an amazing leap forward.

Sheldon, to Leonard, about Howard's date to a Caltech mixer.

Season 1, Episode 4: "The Luminous Fish Effect"
imdb.com

Penny, you don't want to get into it with Sheldon. The guy's one lab accident away from being a super villain.

Leonard, to Penny, after Sheldon disallows Penny from using their apartment Wi-Fi due to the "hamburger incident". (Sheldon getting banned from The Cheesecake Factory.)

Season 2, Episode 7: "The Panty Piñata Polarization"
cbsnews.com, July 18, 2014

Scavenger hunts at Harvard were really tough. I'd always get stuck on the first challenge; trying to find someone to be on a team with me. I guess that story's more sad than funny.

Amy, to the group, about Harvard's famed scavenger hunts, traditions of all the major elite universities (…and Princeton).

Season 7, Episode 3: "The Scavenger Vortex"
"Quotes from 'The Scavenger Vortex'", the-big-bang-theory.com

I'm exceedingly smart.
I graduated college at fourteen.
While my brother was getting
an STD, I was getting a Ph.D.
Penicillin can't take this away.

Sheldon, in his video application to NASA to be one
of the humans considered for the first manned spaceflight
to Mars.

Season 8, Episode 17: "The Colonization Application"
"Best Sheldon Cooper Quotes of All Time", dexerto.com, February 15, 2024

You know, I'm really happy with our wedding date. The month squared equals the square of the sum of the members of the set of prime factors of the day. Isn't that romantic?

Sheldon, to Amy, arranging the couple's impending wedding day. They got married on May 12, FYI. (We think the math checks out.)

Season 11, Episode 17: "The Athenaeum Allocation"
"Amy Farrah Fowler Quotes", the-big-bang-theory.com

How can she remember all those lines, but as a waitress she can't remember 'no tomato' on my hamburger?

Sheldon, watching Penny perform on stage as Blanche DuBois in *A Streetcar Named Desire*, after she returns to amateur acting productions.

Season 6, Episode 17: "The Monster Isolation"
tvfanatic.com, February 22, 2013

Well, there were plenty of things to do before cell phones. I'll look them up… Son of a biscuit!

Sheldon, to Leonard, after they find themselves bored in a department store with bad Wi-Fi reception while the girls shop.

Season 8, Episode 12: "The Space Probe Disintegration"
quotes.net

While I am perfectly happy with the way things are between us, you said that you didn't want to go out with me because I was too smart for you. Well, newsflash, lady. David Underhill is ten times smarter than me. You'd have to drive a railroad spike in his brain for me to beat him at checkers.

Next to him, I am like one of those sign-language gorillas who knows how to ask for grapes. So, my question is... what's up with that? **99**

Leonard, to Penny, about the hot scientist, and colleague of Leonard's who Penny is crushing on. Penny can't believe that David is a physicist: "The physicists I know are indoorsy and pale."

Season 2, Episode 11: "The Bath Item Gift Hypothesis"
imdb.com

Well, I'm a Hindu. My religion teaches that if we suffer in this life, we are rewarded in the next. Three months at the North Pole with Sheldon and I'm reborn as a well-hung billionaire with wings!

Raj, to Howard and Leonard, about his expedition to the North Pole with Sheldon, and if he'll survive that long in isolation with him.

Season 2, Episode 23: "The Monopolar Expedition"
"30 Great Lines From 12 Seasons of *The Big Bang Theory*", cleveland.com, May 11, 2019

$25.5 billion

The estimated NET value of Raj's family fortune. The Koothrappali family's wealth, according to Sheldon, is "about halfway between Bruce Wayne and Scrooge McDuck".

To show our working: the *2011 Forbes Fictional 15* claims Bruce Wayne's wealth at $7 billion and Scrooge McDuck at $44 billion. Later in the series, Raj rejects his father's money to become his own man.

It means I wish you weren't going.

Penny, to herself, after Leonard closes the door and leaves for his three-month-long North Pole expedition.

Season 2, Episode 23: "The Monopolar Expedition"
tvgag.com

I don't have to take this. I'm going to go home and have sex with my husband right now! Maybe I'll let him do it to me in a parking spot, which sounds dirty, but I didn't mean it that way!

Bernadette, to Amy and Penny, after the three girls exchange increasingly mean words over the reassignment of Sheldon's parking spot to Howard.

Season 6, Episode 9: "The Parking Lot Escalation"
tvtropes.org

As long as things keep going great between us, you'll keep asking me to marry you and eventually I'm gonna end up saying yes then we're going to be married forever and the whole thing just freaks me out.

Penny, to Leonard, discussing the seemingly freaky progression, and inevitability, of their rather normal relationship.

Season 6, Episode 16: "The Tangible Affection Proof"
"The Big Bang Theory, Season 6", quotes.net

Oh, please, that's just a piece of paper. This is a piece of paper *and* a medal.

Sheldon, to Amy, after she tells him that their names are already linked together forever via their marriage, regardless of their Nobel Prize medal win.

Season 12, Episode 23: "The Change Constant"
tvfanatic.com, May 17, 2019

Hello, female children. Allow me to inspire you with a story about a great female scientist. Polish-born, French-educated Madame Curie. Co-discoverer of radioactivity. She was a hero of science until her hair fell out, her vomit and stool became full of blood, and she was poisoned to death by her own discovery.

With a little hard work, I see no reason why that can't also happen to any of you. 🙵🙵

Sheldon, to a group of young, female, junior high school students, in a lecture presented by him. He does nothing to inspire them to become scientists.

Season 6, Episode 18: "The Contractual Obligation Implementation"
"Sheldon Cooper Quotes", the-big-bang-theory.com

66

There's no denying I have feelings for you that can't be explained in any other way. I briefly considered that I had a brain parasite. But that seems even more far-fetched. The only conclusion was love.

99

Sheldon, to Amy, telling her he loves her for the first time in his own sweet, sexy Sheldon way.

Season 8, Episode 8: "The Prom Equivalency"
"*The Big Bang Theory* Recap: Prom Night", vulture.com, November 7, 2014

I'm stimulating the pleasures of this starfish. I just need to turn it off. If I don't, then I have to sit through lunch knowing this starfish is having a better day than I am.

Amy, to Penny, discussing one of the least satisfying aspects of her role as a neurobiologist.

Season 8, Episode 2: "The Junior Professor Solution"
"Amy Farrah Fowler Quotes", the-big-bang-theory.com

> 66

I didn't understand *The Big Bang Theory* when we did it the first time. I didn't understand the characters and we had to fail with them to understand how naive and vulnerable they were. Their brilliance hid the fact that, in many ways, they were children and they were very easily hurt. So, when we did it a second time, we incorporated that information. We knew that the audience was going to be protective toward them, and rightly so. Even toward Sheldon, who, despite his arrogance, was very childish and so vulnerable in the world.

> 99

Chuck Lorre,
on having to re-write the characters and pilot episode before receiving a series order, interview with Lisa Campbell, Royal Television Society, July 19, 2017

What do you say to a graduate of the U.C. Berkeley Physics Department? 'I'll have fries with that.' Because his education hasn't prepared him for a career in the sciences.

Sheldon, to Leonard, writing a joke in advance of their upcoming lecture to inspire Berkeley students. Penny whispers to Leonard: "You know, when they chase you out of there, you only have to run faster than Sheldon."

Season 8, Episode 19: "The Skywalker Incursion"
imdb.com

I'm sorry, but this is important… *Back to the Future 2* was in the *Back to the Future 3* case, and *Back to the Future 3* was – get this – in the *Back to the Future 2* case.

Sheldon, to Leonard, over a call while Leonard was on a three-month research expedition in the North Sea with Professor Stephen Hawking.

Season 7, Episode 1: "The Hofstadter Insufficiency"
"The Big Bang Theory, Season 7", quotes.net

❝
We can, but thanks to Steve Jobs, we don't have to. ❞

Sheldon, to Amy, while the group were sitting silently on the sofa, concentrating on their phones. Amy asks: "Can we maybe put the phones down and have an actual human conversation?"

Season 7, Episode 12: "The Hesitation Ramification"
tvfanatic.com, January 3, 2014

Soft kitty, warm kitty, little ball of fur. Happy kitty, sleepy kitty, purr, purr, purr.

Sheldon, singing softly to Amy, to reassure her feelings of "impostor syndrome", after the publication of their Nobel Prize-shortlisted super-asymmetry paper.

Season 12, Episode 19: "The Inspiration Deprivation"
"Legal Fight Erupts Over *Big Bang Theory*'s 'Soft Kitty' Song", deadline.com, December 28, 2015

It's like we have these holes in our lives, but now we fill each other's holes.

Raj, to Howard, about Stuart, who took Howard's place while he was up in space. Howard was clearly jealous of Stuart and Raj's new closeness.

Season 6, Episode 4: "The Re-Entry Minimization"
"*The Big Bang Theory*, Season 6", quotes.net

Thanks, Sheldon. I haven't told my parents yet, but thanks.

Penny, to Sheldon, as he outs her pregnancy in public during his Nobel Prize speech.

Season 12, Episode 24: "The Stockholm Syndrome"
"*The Big Bang Theory*: Each Main Character's First & Last Line In The Series", screenrant.com, January 14, 2021

What do Sheldon Cooper and a black hole have in common? They both suck. Neener-neener-neener!

Professor Stephen Hawking's "brainteaser" to Sheldon, after Hawking calls Sheldon on the phone to ridicule him. Sick burn.

Season 6, Episode 7: "The Extract Obliteration"
"*Big Bang Theory* react: Stephen Hawking lends his voice", ew.com, November 2, 2012

The leaving of a message is one half of a social contract which is completed by the checking of the message. If that contract breaks down then all social contracts break down and we descend into anarchy!

Sheldon, to Leonard, after Leonard refuses to check a message from Stuart Bloom, assuming it's about Penny dating Stuart. Leonard replies, "It must be hell inside your head."

Season 2, Episode 22: "The Classified Materials Turbulence"
imdb.com

You know, I'm given to understand that there's an entire city in Nevada designed specifically to help people like Howard forget their problems and replace them with new problems such as alcoholism, gambling addiction and sexually transmitted diseases.

Sheldon, to Raj, about the vices and virtues of Las Vegas. Raj responds: "Is it me… or is that Sheldon's way of saying 'Vegas Baby'?"

Season 2, Episode 21: "The Vegas Renormalization"
"The Big Bang Theory, Season 2", quotes.net

You told me 'it's mind blowing'.
So, my mind goes into it 'pre-blown'.
Once your mind is 'pre-blown',
it cannot be 're-blown'.

Sheldon, to Stuart Bloom, regarding the – spoiler alert! – quality of the new edition of *Hellboy*. To be fair, Sheldon's got a point. Nobody likes a pre-blown mind.

Season 2, Episode 22: "The Classified Materials Turbulence"
tvfanatic.com, May 5, 2009

Think about it, Sheldon. I'm not a stranger. We're intellectually compatible. I'm willing to chauffeur you around town. And your personality quirks which others find abhorrent or rage-inducing I find cute as a button. What do you think?

Amy, to Sheldon, outlining all the reasons why she is the perfect roommate for him and why they should consider living together.

Season 6, Episode 15: "The Spoiler Alert Segmentation"
"Big Bang Theory: More Cooperisms from Season 6", funtrivia.com, December 3, 2021

CHAPTER
FIVE

THE BIG BANG LEGACY EVALUATION

Future civilizations will look back at the opening decade of the 21st century and marvel at the fact that it was the moment when the world stopped being so analog about everything.

The Big Bang Theory represents that shift and captures it for posterity, magnifying all of society's modern anxieties, peculiarities and foibles through the telescopic lens of six super-smart scientists (and one girl next-door) who, despite their intelligence, only just managed to work out what life is all about: love and friendship…

THE *BIG BANG* LEGACY EVALUATION

Everything is just sex with you, isn't it?

Sheldon, to Amy, after Amy innocently tells Sheldon it's a "beautiful night" and invites her boyfriend to take a walk with her.

Season 7, Episode 10: "The Discovery Dissipation"
"The Big Bang Theory: 'The Discovery Dissipation'", avclub.com, December 6, 2013

I'll just Google 'hot, dark and moist' and see what comes up. Oh, there look, there's all sorts of videos.

Sheldon, to Raj, discussing whether they could survive a dark-matter research expedition in a salt mine by simulating the conditions in a steam tunnel.

Season 8, Episode 6: "The Expedition Approximation"
"*The Big Bang Theory* recap: 'The Expedition Approximation'", ew.com, October 21, 2014

❝ It's annoying when you do it. ❞

Sheldon, to Penny, when Penny knocks on Sheldon's apartment door in the same (now-iconic) obsessive compulsive way that Sheldon knocks on Penny's apartment door.

Season 11, Episode 13: "The Solo Oscillation"
"Sheldon Cooper Quotes", the-big-bang-theory.com

The origin of Sheldon's iconic goofy catchphrase – "Bazinga!" – was first mentioned in *The Big Bang Theory* multiverse in *Young Sheldon*, more specifically, in the episode "A Stunted Childhood and a Can of Fancy Mixed Nuts".

In real-life, the phrase came from one of the writers, Stephen Engel, who constantly played practical jokes on the cast and crew. "If it's funny, it's a Bazinga!" creator/producer Bill Prady told an audience at PaleyFest 2013: "It was Stephen's word for 'Gotcha!'"

I like a party as much as the next man. As long as the next man doesn't like a party.

Sheldon, to Leonard, after Leonard tells Sheldon that his attendance at a party implies that it is not a party.

Season 9, Episode 21: "The Viewing Party Combustion"
imdb.com

Sweetie, every night you don't kill him in his sleep, he wins.

Penny, to Leonard, about Sheldon's itchy and uncomfortable sweater and the principle at stake if he takes it off.

Season 7, Episode 8: "The Itchy Brain Simulation"
"The Big Bang Theory: Penny's 10 Shadiest Burns, Ranked", screenrant.com, November 28, 2020

You'd better find my husband's mother, 'cause one way or another, we're walkin' out of this airport with a dead woman!

Bernadette, to the female lost luggage airport staff member, after the airline lose the urn containing the ashes of Mrs. Wolowitz.

Season 8, Episode 16: "The Intimacy Acceleration"
imdb.com

Good news, gentlemen! Amy's at a conference this weekend, which means I'm available to be entertained. As today's youth might put it, who wants to get their Sheld-on?

Sheldon, to Raj, Leonard and Howard, after finding himself free from boyfriend obligations to Amy all weekend. There were few takers to his request.

Season 9, Episode 12: "The Sales Call Sublimation"
"Sheldon Cooper Quotes", the-big-bang-theory.com

So anyway, to make a long story short, turns out I have an unusually firm cervix.

Amy, to Penny, after being invited to participate in "girl talk". It prompts Penny to reply: "You know, Amy, when we say girl talk, that just doesn't have to be about our lady parts."

Season 4, Episode 8: "The 21-Second Excitation"
"The Big Bang Theory, Season 4", quotes.net

The only thing I've learned in the last two hours is that American men love drinking beer, pee too often and have trouble getting erections.

Raj, to Leonard, after watching American football on TV with Leonard. Though, Raj's attention was more focused on the copious amounts of advertisements in between play.

Season 3, Episode 5: "The Cornhusker Vortex"
tvfanatic.com, November 3, 2009

The X-Men were named for the 'X' in Charles Xavier. Since I'm Sheldon Cooper, you will be my C-Men.

Sheldon, to Penny, after she asks if the group are worthy enough to be Sheldon's X-Men to help overcome his stage fright to accept an academic award.

Season 3, Episode 18: "The Pants Alternative"
"*The Big Bang Theory*: 20 Best Quotes", telegraph.co.uk, October 23, 2014

If that was slang, I'm unfamiliar with it. If it was literal, I share your aversion to soiled hosiery. In any case, I'm here because my mother and I have agreed that I will date at least once a year.

Amy, to Sheldon, upon meeting him for the first time. Sheldon mentioned he only agreed to the date as he was "being blackmailed with a hidden dirty sock".

Season 3, Episode 23: "The Lunar Excitation"
"Sheldon Cooper Quotes", the-big-bang-theory.com

It's okay, I don't mind hearing about your sex life, it's Howard's that bugs me.

Raj, to Leonard, when Leonard wants the group to ask him about his plans.

Season 3, Episode 15: "The Large Hadron Collision"
"*The Big Bang Theory*, Season 3", quotes.net

You went out in the hallway, stumbled into an inter-dimensional portal which brought you 5,000 years into the future where you took advantage of the advanced technology to build a time machine, and now you're back to bring us all with you to the year 7010 where we are transported to work at the thinkatorium by telepathically controlled flying dolphins?

Sheldon, to Leonard, answering, literally, Leonard's rhetorical statement: "You'll never guess what just happened!"*

Season 4, Episode 9: "The Boyfriend Complexity"
"Best Sheldon Cooper Quotes of All Time", ibtimes.co.in, March 24, 2015

* Penny kissed him.

Advanced Intelligence

While the main characters all have below-average EQs (except for Penny), the scientists and physicists all have exceptional IQs.

But whose is the highest?

A genius IQ is anything over 150.
An average IQ is between 90 and 120.

1. **187 Sheldon**
2. **180 Amy**
3. **175 Raj**
4. **173 Leonard**
5. **170 Barry (Kripke)**
6. **160 Bernadette**
7. **140 Howard**
8. **120 Beverly (Hofstadter)**
9. **110 Penny**
10. **100 Stuart (Bloom)**

'Who's Adam West?'
Leonard, what do the two of you
talk about after coitus?

Sheldon, to Penny, after Penny makes it clear that
she doesn't know who Adam West is. He is the actor who,
famously, was the first to put on the cowl and cape in
Batman in the 1960s.

Season 3, Episode 17: "The Precious Fragmentation"
"*Big Bang Theory* recap: One ring to rule them all", ew.com, March 9, 2010

To paraphrase Shakespeare,
'It's better to have loved and lost than
to stay home every night and
download increasingly shameful
pornography'.

Raj, to Penny, after Penny admits that she should have
never split up with Leonard.

Season 4, Episode 23: "The Roommate Transmogrification"
"*The Big Bang Theory*: 10 Funniest Raj Quotes About Love" screenrant.com,
January 28, 2020

Penny, while I subscribe to the 'Many Worlds' theory, which posits the existence of an infinite number of Sheldons in an infinite number of universes, I assure you that in none of them am I dancing.

Sheldon, to Penny, rejecting her invitation to dance with her. The "Many Worlds" theory is a philosophical position about how the mathematics used in quantum mechanics relates to physical reality. Put simply: everything happens everywhere all at once.

Season 3, Episode 1: "The Gothowitz Deviation"
"*The Big Bang Theory*: Funniest Quotes", 93qcountry.com, September 23, 2021

Yes. In 1917 when Albert Einstein established the theoretic foundation for the laser in his paper 'Quantentheorie der Strahlung', his fondest hope was that the resultant device be 'bitchin'.

Sheldon, to Zack Johnson, Penny's new boyfriend, who believes lasers to be "bitchin".

Season 3, Episode 23: "The Lunar Excitation"
tvfanatic.com, May 25, 2010

Please don't take this the wrong way, but I would rather swim butt-naked across the Ganges with a paper cut on my nipple, and then die a slow agonizing death from viral infection, than work with you.

Raj, to Sheldon, about the possibility of working with Sheldon. Correction: working for Sheldon.

Season 3, Episode 4: "The Pirate Solution"
"Top 15 Put-Downs from *The Big Bang Theory*", dstv.com, June 17, 2015

His right hand is calling him?

Penny, to Howard, after he checks the caller ID and exclaims proudly, "Ooh, looks like I'm gonna have sex tonight!"

Season 2, Episode 16: "The Cushion Saturation"
"Penny Quotes", the-big-bang-theory.com

The problem isn't what's on the inside, it's the creepy candy coating.

Penny, to Leonard, about Howard, after Leonard insists that Howard is a good guy on the inside.

Season 3, Episode 5: "The Creepy Candy Coating Corollary"
quotational.com

That is a trick question. The answer is: you as the groom.

Leonard, to Sheldon, after Sheldon asks him: "What do you think will make the wedding worse for Amy: a cake made with salt instead of sugar or a cake iced with congealed gravy?

Season 11, Episode 10: "The Confidence Erosion"
imdb.com